ISBN 0 86112 825 7
© Brimax Books Ltd 1992. All rights reserved.
Published by Brimax Books Ltd, Newmarket, England 1992.
Printed in Italy.

A
Children's Book
of Verse

ILLUSTRATED BY
Eric Kincaid

BRIMAX BOOKS • NEWMARKET • ENGLAND

Introduction

A Children's Book of Verse is a beautiful selection of poetry that will be treasured by all who read it. Timeless classics as well as modern day verse abound, creating a book that changes constantly; one second happy, the next sad and with a turn of the page, full of laughter.

From William Blake to Spike Milligan, *A Children's Book of Verse* is a joy to read. The superb illustrations by Eric Kincaid bring warmth and richness to every page, and the endless variety of verse will enchant old and young alike, stirring the imagination and never ceasing to entertain.

Acknowledgements

We wish to thank the following for permission to use copyright poems:

Norman Ault: *The Pig's Tail*, from *Dreamland Stories* (1920) by permission of Oxford University Press. **Walter de la Mare:** *Someone*, by permission of the Literary Trustees of Walter de la Mare and the Society of Authors as their representative. **Eleanor Farjeon:** *Cat! A Kitten*, published by Michael Joseph by permission of David Higham Associates Ltd. **Rose Fyleman:** *The Balloon Man, Fairies*, by permission of the Society of Authors as the Literary Representative of the estate of Rose Fyleman. **Percy H. Illot:** *The Witch*, from *Songs of English Childhood*, by permission of J.M. Dent and Sons Ltd. **James Kirkup:** *Kitten in the Falling Snow, The Lonely Scarecrow*, from *Refusal to Conform* by permission of Mr James Kirkup and Oxford University Press. **Roger McGough:** *Mrs Moon*, from *Sky in the Pie* reprinted by permission of A.D. Peters and Co Ltd. **Spike Milligan:** *On the Ning Nang Nong*, by permission of Spike Milligan Productions Ltd. **Ogden Nash** *The Duck*, from *Verses from 1929 On* © 1936 by the Curtis Publishing Company, first appeared in the Saturday Evening Post, by permission of Andre Deutsch Ltd and Little Brown and Co, Boston USA. **Jack Prelutsky:** *The Hippopotamus*, from *Zoo Doings* © 1970, 1983 by Jack Prelutsky by permission of Greenwillow Books (a division of William Morrow and Company. **Alexander Resnikoff:** *Two Witches* from *Oh, How Silly!* by permission of Laurence Pollinger Ltd. **Ian Serrailler:** *The Squirrel*, from *A Puffin Quartet of Poems* 1944, 1958 © Ian Serrailler, Puffin Books Ltd. **Gabriel Setoun:** *Jack Frost*, by permission of The Bodley Head Ltd, from *The Child World* by Gabriel Setoun. **Stevie Smith:** *Fairy Story*, from *The Collected Poems* © 1972 by Stevie Smith (Penguin Modern Classics) by permission of James MacGibbon as the Literary Executor and by permission of New Directions Publishing Corp. **Marjorie Wilson:** *The Little Things that Happen*, by permission of Basil Blackwell.

Every effort has been made to trace the copyright holders but this has not been possible in every case. The publishers apologise to any copyright holders whose rights have been unwittingly infringed.

Contents

A Kitten

He's nothing much but fur
And two round eyes of blue,
He has a giant purr
And a midget mew.

He darts and pats the air,
He starts and pricks his ear,
When there is nothing there
For him to see and hear.

He runs around in rings,
But why we cannot tell;
With sideways leap he springs
At things invisible—

Then half-way through a leap
His startled eyeballs close,
And he drops off to sleep
With one paw on his nose.

Eleanor Farjeon

Washing

What is all this washing about,
Every day, week in, week out?
From getting up till going to bed,
I'm tired of hearing the same thing said.
Whether I'm dirty or whether I'm not,
Whether the water is cold or hot,
Whether I like or whether I don't,
Whether I will or whether I won't —
'Have you washed your hands, and washed your face?'
I seem to *live* in the washing-place.

Whenever I go for a walk or ride,
As soon as I put my nose inside
The door again, there's some one there
With a sponge and soap, and a lot they care
If I have something better to do,
'Now wash your face and your fingers too.'

Before a meal is ever begun,
And after ever a meal is done,
It's time to turn on the waterspout.
Please, what *is* all this washing about?

John Drinkwater

My Shadow

I have a little shadow that goes in and out with me,
And what can be the use of him is more than I can see.
He is very, very like me from the heels up to the head;
And I see him jump before me, when I jump into my bed.

The funniest thing about him is the way he likes to grow—
Not at all like proper children, which is always very slow:
For he sometimes shoots up taller like an india-rubber ball,
And he sometimes gets so little that there's none of him
    at all.

He hasn't got a notion of how children ought to play,
And can only make a fool of me in every sort of way.
He stays so close beside me, he's a coward you can see;
I'd think shame to stick to nursie as that shadow sticks
    to me!

One morning, very early, before the sun was up,
I rose and found the shining dew on every buttercup;
But my lazy little shadow, like an arrant sleepy-head,
Had stayed at home behind me and was fast asleep
    in bed.

Robert Louis Stevenson

The Big Rock Candy Mountains

On a summer's day in the month of May,
A burly bum come a-hiking,
Travelling down that lonesome road
A-looking for his liking.
He was headed for a land that was far away,
Beside them crystal fountains—
'I'll see you all this coming fall
In the Big Rock Candy Mountains.'

In the Big Rock Candy Mountains
You never change your socks,
And little streams of alcohol
Come a-trickling down the rocks.
The box cars are all empty
And the railroad bulls are blind,
There's a lake of stew and whisky, too,
You can paddle all around 'em in a big canoe
In the Big Rock Candy Mountains.

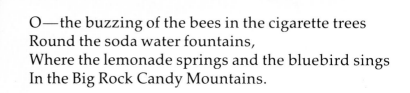

O—the buzzing of the bees in the cigarette trees
Round the soda water fountains,
Where the lemonade springs and the bluebird sings
In the Big Rock Candy Mountains.

In the Big Rock Candy Mountains,
There's a land that's fair and bright,
Where the hand-outs grow on bushes
And you sleep out every night,
Where the box cars are all empty
And the sun shines every day,
O I'm bound to go, where there ain't no snow,
Where the rain don't fall and the wind don't blow
In the Big Rock Candy Mountains.

In the Big Rock Candy Mountains
The jails are made of tin
And you can bust right out again
As soon as they put you in;
The farmers' trees are full of fruit,
The barns are full of hay,
I'm going to stay where you sleep all day,
Where they boiled in oil the inventor of toil
In the Big Rock Candy Mountains.

Anonymous

13

My Dog, Spot

I have a white dog
Whose name is Spot,
And he's sometimes white
And he's sometimes not.
But whether he's white
Or whether he's not,
There's a patch on his ear
That makes him Spot.

He has a tongue
That is long and pink,
And he lolls it out
When he wants to think.
He seems to think most
When the weather is hot
He's a wise sort of dog,
Is my dog, Spot.

He likes a bone
And he likes a ball,
But he doesn't care
For a cat at all.
He waggles his tail
And he knows what's what,
So I'm glad that he's my dog,
My dog, Spot.

Rodney Bennett

Who Has Seen the Wind?

Who has seen the wind?
Neither I nor you:
But when the leaves hang trembling,
The wind is passing through.

Who has seen the wind?
Neither you nor I:
But when the trees bow down their heads,
The wind is passing by.

Christina Rossetti

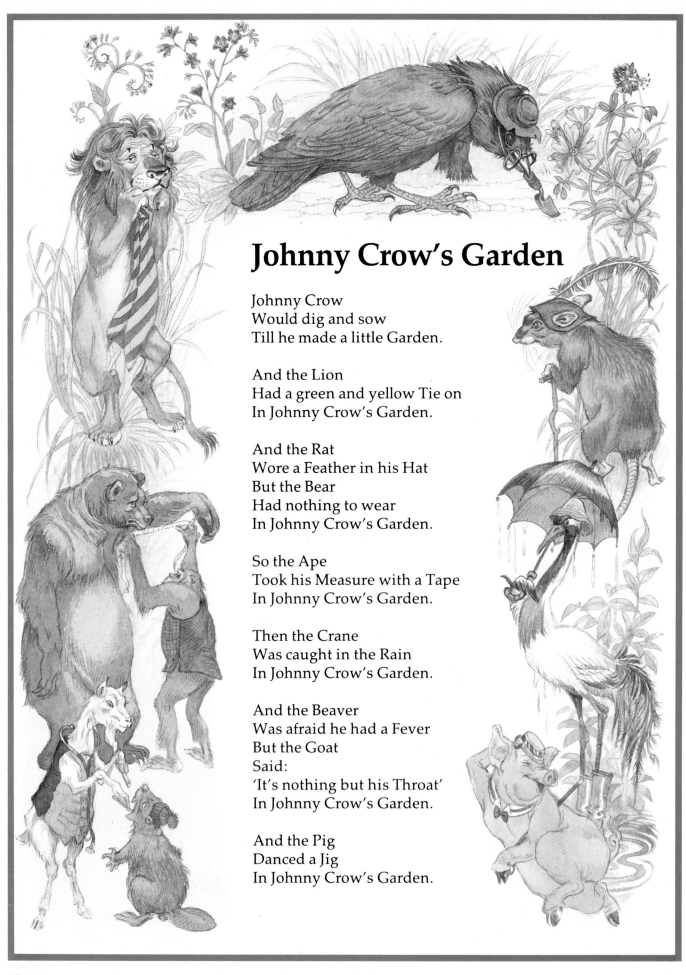

Johnny Crow's Garden

Johnny Crow
Would dig and sow
Till he made a little Garden.

And the Lion
Had a green and yellow Tie on
In Johnny Crow's Garden.

And the Rat
Wore a Feather in his Hat
But the Bear
Had nothing to wear
In Johnny Crow's Garden.

So the Ape
Took his Measure with a Tape
In Johnny Crow's Garden.

Then the Crane
Was caught in the Rain
In Johnny Crow's Garden.

And the Beaver
Was afraid he had a Fever
But the Goat
Said:
'It's nothing but his Throat'
In Johnny Crow's Garden.

And the Pig
Danced a Jig
In Johnny Crow's Garden.

Then the Stork
Gave a Philosophic Talk
Till the Hippopotami
Said: 'Ask no further "What am I?"'
While the Elephant
Said something quite irrelevant
In Johnny Crow's Garden.

And the Goose—
Well,
The Goose *was* a Goose
In Johnny Crow's Garden.

And the Mouse
Built himself a little House
Where the Cat
Sat down beside the Mat
In Johnny Crow's Garden.

And the Whale
Told a very long Tale
In Johnny Crow's Garden.

And the Owl
Was a funny old Fowl
And the Fox
Put them all in the Stocks
In Johnny Crow's Garden.

But Johnny Crow
He let them go
And they all sat down
To their dinner in a row
In Johnny Crow's Garden!

L. Leslie Brooke

The Frog and the Bird

By a quiet little stream on an old mossy log,
Looking very forlorn, sat a little green frog;
He'd a sleek speckled back, and two bright yellow eyes,
And when dining, selected the choicest of flies.

The sun was so hot he scarce opened his eyes,
Far too lazy to stir, let alone watch for flies,
He was nodding, and nodding, and almost asleep,
When a voice in the branches chirped: 'Froggie, cheep,
   cheep!'

'You'd better take care,' piped the bird to the frog,
'In the water you'll be if you fall off that log.
Can't you see that the streamlet is up to the brim?'
Croaked the froggie: 'What odds! You forget I can swim!'

Then the froggie looked up at the bird perched so high
On a bough that to him seemed to reach to the sky;
So he croaked to the bird: 'If you fall, you will die!'
Chirped the birdie: 'What odds! You forget I can fly!'

Vera Hessey

The Pig's Tail

A furry coat has the bear to wear,
   The tortoise a coat of mail,
The yak has more than his share of hair,
   But—the pig has the curly tail.

The elephant's tusks are sold for gold,
   The slug leaves a silver trail,
The parrot is never too old to scold,
   But—the pig has a curly tail.

The lion can either roar or snore,
   The cow gives milk in a pail,
The dog can guard a door, and more,
   But—the pig has the curly tail.

The monkey makes you smile a while,
   The tiger makes you quail,
The fox has many a wile of guile,
   But—the pig has the curly tail.

For the rest of the beasts that prey or play,
   From tiny mouse to the whale,
There's much that I could say today,
   But—the pig has the curly tail.

Norman Ault

Fairies

There are fairies at the bottom of our garden!
   It's not so very, very far away;
You pass the gardener's shed and you just keep
   straight ahead—
   I do so hope they've really come to stay.
There's a little wood, with moss in it and beetles,
   And a little stream that quietly runs through;
You wouldn't think they'd dare to come merry-making
   there—
      Well, they do.

There are fairies at the bottom of our garden!
   They often have a dance on summer nights;
The butterflies and bees make a lovely little breeze,
   And the rabbits stand about and hold the lights.
Did you know that they could sit upon the moonbeams
   And pick a little star to make a fan,
And dance away up there in the middle of the air?
      Well, they can.

20

There are fairies at the bottom of our garden!
   You cannot think how beautiful they are;
They all stand up and sing when the Fairy Queen and King
   Come gently floating down upon their car.
The King is very proud and *very* handsome;
   The Queen—now can you guess who that could be
(She's a little girl all day, but at night she steals away)?
      Well—it's Me!

Rose Fyleman

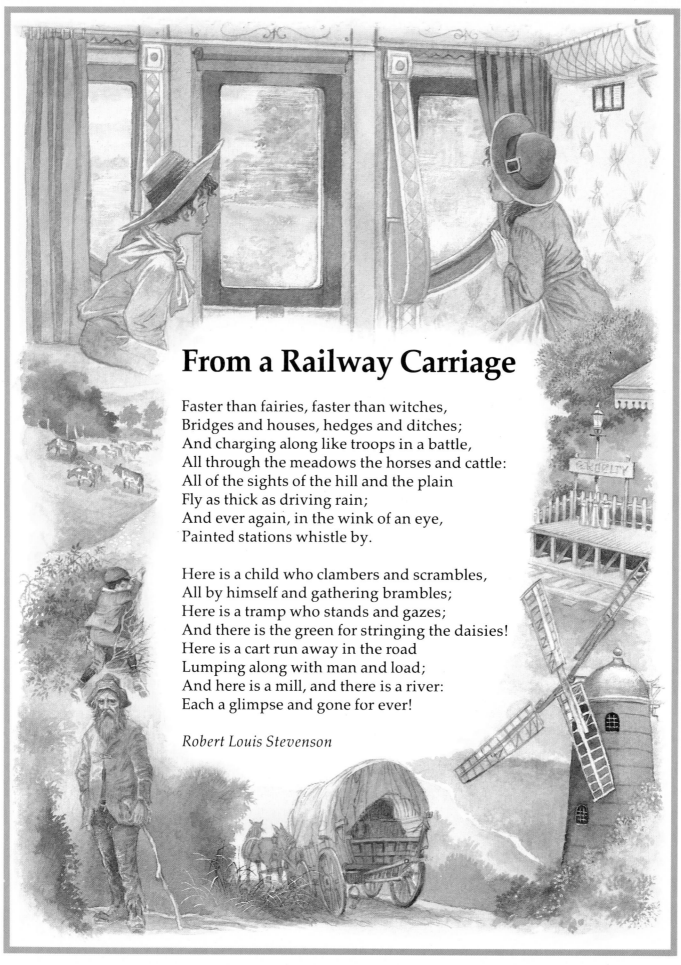

From a Railway Carriage

Faster than fairies, faster than witches,
Bridges and houses, hedges and ditches;
And charging along like troops in a battle,
All through the meadows the horses and cattle:
All of the sights of the hill and the plain
Fly as thick as driving rain;
And ever again, in the wink of an eye,
Painted stations whistle by.

Here is a child who clambers and scrambles,
All by himself and gathering brambles;
Here is a tramp who stands and gazes;
And there is the green for stringing the daisies!
Here is a cart run away in the road
Lumping along with man and load;
And here is a mill, and there is a river:
Each a glimpse and gone for ever!

Robert Louis Stevenson

An Eskimo Baby

If you were an Eskimo baby
You'd live in a bag all day.
    Right up from your toes
    To the tip of your nose,
All in thick cosy furs tucked away.

And if you went out for an airing
In mother's warm hood you would go,
    Tied close to her back,
    Like a soft, furry pack,
You could laugh at the cold and the snow.

But if they brought water at bedtime—
As people at home always do—
    You'd cough and you'd sneeze,
    And perhaps you would freeze,
You would certainly turn very blue!

An Eskimo mummy would rub you
With oil from your heels to your head.
    And then you'd be rolled
    (For it's terribly cold)
In warm furs, and put safely to bed.

No nice creamy milk for your supper,
But bits of raw blubber and fat!
    Would you like to go
    To the land of the snow,
Where they have such a bedtime as that?

Lucy Diamond

Mrs Moon

Mrs Moon
sitting up in the sky
Little Old Lady
rock-a-bye
with a ball of fading light
and silvery needles
knitting the night.

Roger McGough

If You Should Meet a Crocodile

If you should meet a crocodile,
Don't take a stick and poke him;
Ignore the welcome in his smile,
Be careful not to stroke him.

For as he sleeps upon the Nile,
He thinner gets and thinner;
And whene'er you meet a crocodile
He's ready for his dinner.

Anonymous

Way Down South Where Bananas Grow

Way down south where bananas grow,
A grasshopper stepped on an elephant's toe.
The elephant said, with tears in his eyes,
'Pick on somebody your own size.'

Anonymous

The Little Things That Happen

The Little Things That Happen
  Are tucked into your mind,
And come again to greet you
  (Or most of them, you'll find).

Through many little doorways,
  Of which you keep the keys,
They crowd into your thinking—
  We call them Memories.

But some of them are rovers
  And wander off and get
So lost, the keys grow rusty,
  And that means—you forget.

But some stay ever near you;
  You'll find they never rove—
The keys are always shining—
  Those are the things you love.

Marjorie Wilson

The Butterfly's Ball

Come take up your hats, and away let us haste
To the butterfly's ball and the grasshopper's feast;
The trumpeter gadfly has summoned the crew,
And the revels are now only waiting for you.
On the smooth shaven grass, by the side of the wood,
Beneath a broad oak that for ages has stood,
See the children of earth, and the tenants of air,
For an evening's amusement together repair.

And there came the beetle so blind and so black,
Who carried the emmet, his friend, on his back;
And there was the gnat, and the dragon-fly too,
With all their relations, green, orange, and blue.

And there came the moth in his plumage of down,
And the hornet in jacket of yellow and brown,
Who with him the wasp his companion did bring,
But they promised that evening to lay by their sting.

And the sly little dormouse crept out of his hole,
And led to the feast his blind brother the mole,
And the snail, with his horns peeping out from
     his shell,
Came from a great distance—the length of an ell.

A mushroom their table, and on it was laid
A water-dock leaf, which a table-cloth made;
The viands were various, to each of their taste,
And the bee brought his honey to crown the repast.

There, close on his haunches, so solemn and wise,
The frog from a corner looked up to the skies;
And the squirrel, well pleased such diversions to see,
Sat cracking his nuts overhead in a tree.

Then out came the spider, with fingers so fine,
To show his dexterity on the tight line;
From one branch to another his cobwebs he slung,
Then, quick as an arrow, he darted along.

But just in the middle, oh! shocking to tell!
From his rope in an instant poor Harlequin fell;
Yet he touched not the ground, but with talons
    outspread,
Hung suspended in air at the end of a thread.

Then the grasshopper came with a jerk and a spring,
Very long was his leg, though but short was his wing;
He took but three leaps, and was soon out of sight,
Then chirped his own praises the rest of the night.

With step so majestic, the snail did advance,
And promised the gazers a minuet to dance;
But they all laughed so loud that he pulled in his head,
And went in his own little chamber to bed.

Then as evening gave way to the shadows of night
Their watchman, the glowworm, came out with
    his light;
Then home let us hasten while yet we can see,
For no watchman is waiting for you and for me.

William Roscoe

The Lonely Scarecrow

My poor old bones—I've only two—
A broomshank and a broken stave,
My ragged gloves are a disgrace,
My one peg-foot is in the grave.

I wear the labourer's old clothes;
Coat, shirt and trousers all undone.
I bear my cross upon a hill
In rain and shine, in snow and sun.

I cannot help the way I look.
My funny hat is full of hay.
—O, wild birds, come and nest in me!
Why do you always fly away?

James Kirkup

The Rainbow Fairies

Two little clouds, one summer's day,
Went flying through the sky;
They went so fast they bumped their heads,
And both began to cry.

Old Father Sun looked out and said:
'Oh, never mind, my dears,
I'll send my little fairy folk
To dry your falling tears.'

One fairy came in violet,
And one wore indigo;
In blue, green, yellow, orange, red,
They made a pretty row.

They wiped the cloud-tears all away,
And then from out the sky,
Upon a line the sunbeams made,
They hung their gowns to dry.

Anonymous

The Fly-Away Horse

Oh, a wonderful horse is the Fly-Away Horse—
    Perhaps you have seen him before;
Perhaps, while you slept, his shadow has swept
    Through the moonlight that floats on the floor.
For it's only at night, when the stars twinkle bright,
    That the Fly-Away Horse, with a neigh
And a pull at his rein and a toss of his mane,
    Is up on his heels and away!
        The Moon in the sky,
        As he gallopeth by,
    Cries: 'Oh! what a marvellous sight!'
        And the Stars in dismay
        Hide their faces away
    In the lap of old Grandmother Night.

It is yonder, out yonder, the Fly-Away Horse
    Speedeth ever and ever away—
Over meadows and lanes, over mountains and plains,
    Over streamlets that sing at their play;
And over the sea like a ghost sweepeth he,
    While the ships they go sailing below,
And he speedeth so fast that the men at the mast
    Adjudge him some portent of woe.
        'What ho, there!' they cry,
        As he flourishes by
    With a whisk of his beautiful tail;
        And the fish in the sea
        Are as scared as can be,
    From the nautilus up to the whale!

And the Fly-Away Horse seeks those far-away lands
　　You little folk dream of at night—
Where candy-trees grow, and honey-brooks flow,
　　And corn-fields with popcorn are white;
And the beasts in the wood are ever so good
　　To children who visit them there—
What glory astride of a lion to ride,
　　Or to wrestle around with a bear!
　　　　The monkeys, they say:
　　　　'Come on, let us play,'
　　And they frisk in the coconut-trees:
　　　　While the parrots, that cling
　　　　To the peanut-vines, sing
　　Or converse with comparative ease!

Off! scamper to bed—you shall ride him tonight!
　　For, as soon as you've fallen asleep,
With jubilant neigh he shall bear you away
　　Over forest and hillside and deep!
But tell us, my dear, all you see and you hear
　　In those beautiful lands over there,
Where the Fly-Away Horse wings his far-away course
　　With the wee one consigned to his care.
　　　　Then Grandma will cry
　　　　In amazement: 'Oh, my!'
　　And she'll think it could never be so.
　　　　And only we two
　　　　Shall know it is true—
You and I, little precious! shall know!

Eugene Field

Cat!

Cat!
Scat!
Atter her, atter her,
Sleeky flatterer,
Spitfire chatterer,
Scatter her, scatter her
  Off her mat!
  Wuff!
  Wuff!
  Treat her rough!
Git her, git her,
Whiskery spitter!
Catch her, catch her,
Green-eyed scratcher!
  Slathery
  Slithery
  Hisser,
  Don't miss her!
Run till you're dithery,
  Hithery
  Thithery
  Pfitts! Pfitts!
  How she spits!
  Spitch! Spatch!
  Can't she scratch!
Scritching the bark
Of the sycamore-tree,
She's reached her ark
And's hissing at me
  Pfitts! Pfitts!
  Wuff! Wuff!
    Scat,
    Cat!
    That's
    That!

Eleanor Farjeon

32

Two Witches

There was a witch
The witch had an itch
The itch was so itchy it
Gave her a twitch.

Another witch
Admired the twitch
So she started twitching
Though she had no itch.

Now both of them twitch
So it's hard to tell which
Witch has the itch and
Which witch has the twitch.

Alexander Resnikoff

The Song of Mr. Toad

The world has held great Heroes,
    As history books have showed;
But never a name to go down to fame
    Compared with that of Toad!

The clever men at Oxford
    Know all that there is to be knowed,
But they none of them know one half as much
    As intelligent Mr. Toad!

The animals sat in the Ark and cried,
    Their tears in torrents flowed.
Who was it said, 'There's land ahead'?
    Encouraging Mr. Toad!

The Army all saluted
    As they marched along the road.
Was it the King? Or Kitchener?
    No. It was Mr. Toad!

The Queen and her Ladies-in-waiting
    Sat at the window and sewed.
She cried, 'Look! who's that *handsome* man?'
    They answered, 'Mr. Toad.'

Kenneth Grahame

Jack Frost

Look out! look out!
Jack Frost is about!
He's after our fingers and toes;
And, all through the night,
The gay little sprite
Is working where nobody knows.

He'll climb each tree,
So nimble is he,
His silvery powder he'll shake;
To windows he'll creep,
And while we're asleep,
Such wonderful pictures he'll make.

Across the grass
He'll merrily pass,
And change all its greenness to white;
Then home he will go,
And laugh, 'Ho! ho! ho!
What fun I have had in the night!'

Cecily Pike

The Tiger

Tiger! Tiger! burning bright
In the forests of the night,
What immortal hand or eye
Could frame thy fearful symmetry?

In what distant deeps or skies
Burnt the fire of thine eyes?
On what wings dare he aspire?
What the hand dare seize the fire?

And what shoulder, and what art
Could twist the sinews of thy heart?
And, when thy heart began to beat,
What dread hand forged thy dread feet?

What the hammer? what the chain?
In what furnace was thy brain?
What the anvil? what dread grasp
Dare its deadly terrors clasp?

When the stars threw down their spears,
And watered heaven with their tears,
Did he smile his work to see?
Did he who made the Lamb make thee?

Tiger! Tiger! burning bright
In the forests of the night,
What immortal hand or eye
Dare frame thy fearful symmetry?

William Blake

The Sugar-Plum Tree

Have you ever heard of the Sugar-Plum Tree?
   'Tis a marvel of great renown!
It blooms on the shore of the Lollipop sea
   In the garden of Shut-Eye Town;
The fruit that it bears is so wondrously sweet
   (As those who have tasted it say)
That good little children have only to eat
   Of that fruit to be happy next day.

When you've got to the tree, you would have a hard time
   To capture the fruit which I sing;
The tree is so tall that no person could climb
   To the boughs where the sugar-plums swing!
But up in that tree sits a chocolate cat,
   And a gingerbread dog prowls below—
And this is the way you contrive to get at
   Those sugar-plums tempting you so:

You say but the word to that gingerbread dog
   And he barks with such terrible zest
That the chocolate cat is at once all agog,
   As her swelling proportions attest.
And the chocolate cat goes cavorting around
   From this leafy limb unto that,
And the sugar-plums tumble, of course, to the ground—
   Hurrah for that chocolate cat!

There are marshmallows, gumdrops, and peppermint canes
   With stripings of scarlet or gold,
And you carry away of the treasure that rains
   As much as your apron can hold!
So come, little child, cuddle closer to me
   In your dainty white nightcap and gown,
And I'll rock you away to that Sugar-Plum Tree
   In the garden of Shut-Eye Town.

Eugene Field

The Robin

When up aloft
I fly and fly,
I see in pools
The shining sky,
And a happy bird
Am I, am I!

When I descend
Toward the brink
I stand and look
And stop and drink
And bathe my wings,
And chink, and prink.

When winter frost
Makes earth as steel,
I search and search
But find no meal,
And most unhappy
Then I feel.

But when it lasts,
And snows still fall,
I get to feel
No grief at all,
For I turn to a cold, stiff
Feathery ball!

Thomas Hardy

Mr Nobody

I know a funny little man,
  As quiet as a mouse,
Who does the mischief that is done
  In everybody's house!
There's no one ever sees his face,
  And yet we all agree
That every plate we break was cracked
  By Mr Nobody.

'Tis he who always tears our books,
  Who leaves the door ajar,
He pulls the buttons from our shirts,
  And scatters pins afar;
That squeaking door will always squeak
  For, prithee, don't you see,
We leave the oiling to be done
  By Mr Nobody.

He puts damp wood upon the fire,
  That kettles cannot boil;
His are the feet that bring in mud,
  And all the carpets soil.
The papers always are mislaid,
  Who had them last but he?
There's not one tosses them about
  But Mr Nobody.

The finger-marks upon the door
  By none of us are made;
We never leave the blinds unclosed,
  To let the curtains fade;
The ink we never spill; the boots
  That lying round you see
Are not our boots; they all belong
  To Mr Nobody.

Anonymous

The Balloon Man

He always comes on market days,
 And holds balloons—a lovely bunch—
And in the market square he stays,
 And never seems to think of lunch.

They're red and purple, blue and green,
 And when it is a sunny day
Tho' carts and people get between
 You see them shining far away.

And some are big and some are small,
 All tied together with a string,
And if there is a wind at all
 They tug and tug like anything.

Some day perhaps he'll let them go
 And we shall see them sailing high,
And stand and watch them from below—
 They *would* look pretty in the sky!

Rose Fyleman

The Kitten
in the Falling Snow

The year-old kitten
has never seen snow,
fallen or falling, until now
this late winter afternoon.

He sits with wide eyes
at the firelit window, sees
white things falling
from black trees.

Are they petals, leaves or birds?
They cannot be the cabbage whites
he batted briefly with his paws,
or the puffball seeds in summer grass.

They make no sound, they have no wings
and yet they can whirl and fly around
until they swoop like swallows, and
disappear into the ground.

'Where do they go?' he questions,
with eyes ablaze, following their flight
into black stone. So I put him
out into the yard, to make their acquaintance.

He has to look up at them: when one
blanches his coral nose, he sneezes,
and flicks a few from his whiskers, from
his sharpened ear, that picks up silences.

He catches one on a curled-up paw
and licks it quickly, before
its strange milk fades, then sniffs its ghost,
a wetness, while his black coat

shivers with stars of flickering frost.
He shivers at something else that makes his thin
tail swish, his fur stand on end! 'What's this? . . .'
Then he suddenly scoots in to safety

and sits again with wide eyes
at the firelit window, sees
white things falling
from black trees.

James Kirkup

On the Ning Nang Nong

On the Ning Nang Nong
Where the Cows go Bong!
And the Monkeys all say Boo!
There's a Nong Nang Ning
Where the trees go Ping!
And the tea pots Jibber Jabber Joo.
On the Nong Ning Nang
All the mice go Clang!
And you just can't catch 'em when they do!
So it's Ning Nang Nong!
Cows go Bong!
Nong Nang Ning!
Trees go Ping!
Nong Ning Nang!
The mice go Clang!
What a noisy place to belong,
Is the Ning Nang Ning Nang Nong!!

Spike Milligan

Little Trotty Wagtail

Little trotty wagtail, he went in the rain,
And twittering, tottering sideways he ne'er got straight
   again.
He stooped to get a worm, and looked up to get a fly,
And then he flew away ere his feathers they were dry.

Little trotty wagtail, he waddled in the mud,
And he left his little footmarks, trample where
   he would.
He waddled in the water-pudge, and waggle went
   his tail,
And chirrupt up his wings to dry upon the garden rail.

Little trotty wagtail, you nimble all about,
And in the dimpling water-pudge you waddle
   in and out;
Your home is nigh at hand, and in the warm pig-stye,
So little Master Wagtail, I'll bid you a good-bye.

John Clare

Jack Frost

The door was shut, as doors should be,
Before you went to bed last night;
But Jack Frost has got in, you see,
And left your window silver white.

He must have waited till you slept;
And not a single word he spoke,
But pencilled o'er the panes and crept
Away again before you woke.

And now you cannot see the hills
Nor fields that stretch beyond the lane;
But there are fairer things than these
His fingers traced on every pane.

Rocks and castles towering high;
Hills and dales and streams and fields;
And knights in armour riding by,
With nodding plumes and shining shields.

And here are little boats, and there
Big ships with sails spread to the breeze;
And yonder, palm trees waving fair
On islands set in silver seas.

And butterflies with gauzy wings;
And herds of cows and flocks of sheep;
And fruit and flowers and all the things
You see when you are sound asleep.

For creeping softly underneath
The door, when all the lights are out,
Jack Frost takes every breath you breathe
And knows the things you think about.

He paints them on the window pane,
In fairy lines with frozen steam;
And when you wake you see again
The lovely things you saw in dream.

Gabriel Setoun

The Wind

Some one tapped at the window pane
　　A little while ago.
Some one runs around the house,
　　And whistles loud and low.
Some one shakes the garden gate,
　　And climbs the garden wall.
Yet when I say:—'Who's that out there?'
　　It's nobody at all.
He's calling down the chimney now,
　　With quite a noisy roar;
He's piping through the key-hole,
　　And he's knocking on the door.
'Come in! Come in!' But no one comes.
　　I peep into the hall,
And though I feel a puff of wind,
　　There's no one there at all.

John Lea

Ducks' Ditty

All along the backwater,
Through the rushes tall,
Ducks are a-dabbling,
Up tails all!

Ducks' tails, drakes' tails,
Yellow feet a-quiver,
Yellow bills all out of sight
Busy in the river!

Slushy green undergrowth
Where the roach swim—
Here we keep our larder,
Cool and full and dim.

Every one for what he likes!
We like to be
Heads down, tails up,
Dabbling free!

High in the blue above
Swifts whirl and call—
We are down a-dabbling,
Up tails all!

Kenneth Grahame

The Squirrel

Among the fox-red fallen leaves I surprised him. Snap
Up the chestnut bole he leapt,
The brown leaper, clawing up-swept:
Turned on the first bough and scolded me roundly.
That's right, load me with reviling,
Spit at me, swear horrible, shame me if you can.
But scared of my smiling
Off and up he scurries. Now Jack's up the beanstalk
Among the dizzy giants. He skips
Along the highest branches, along
Tree-fingers slender as string,
Fur tail following, to the very tips:
Then leaps the aisle—
Oh fear he fall
A hundred times his little length!
He's over! clings, swings on a spray,
Then lightly, the ghost of a mouse, against the sky traces
For me his runway of rare wonder, races
Helter-skelter without pause or break
(I think of the snail—how long would he take?)
On and onward, not done yet—
His errand? Some nut-plunder, you bet.
Oh he's gone!
I peer and search and strain for him, but he's gone.

I wait and watch at the giants' feet, among
The fox-red fallen leaves. One drop
Of rain lands with a smart tap
On the drum, on parchment leaf. I wait
And wait and shiver and forget . . .

A fancy: suppose these trees, so ancient, so
Venerable, so rock-rooted, suddenly
Heaved up their huge elephantine hooves
(O the leaves, how they'd splutter and splash
Like a waterfall, a red waterfall)—suppose
They trudged away!
What would the squirrel say?

Ian Serraillier

The Witch

I saw her plucking cowslips,
And marked her where she stood:
She never knew I watched her
While hiding in the wood.

Her skirt was brightest crimson,
And black her steeple hat,
Her broomstick lay beside her—
I'm positive of that.

Her chin was sharp and pointed,
Her eyes were—I don't know—
For, when she turned towards me—
I thought it best—to go!

Percy H. Ilott

Someone

Someone came knocking
At my wee, small door;
Someone came knocking,
I'm sure—sure—sure;
I listened, I opened,
I looked to left and right,
But nought there was a-stirring
In the still dark night.
Only the busy beetle
Tap-tapping in the wall,
Only from the forest
The screech-owl's call,
Only the cricket whistling
While the dewdrops fall,
So I know not who came knocking,
At all, at all, at all.

Walter de la Mare

The Lobster Quadrille

'Will you walk a little faster?'
Said a whiting to a snail,
'There's a porpoise close behind us,
And he's treading on my tail.
See how eagerly the lobsters
And the turtles all advance!
They are waiting on the shingle—
Will you come and join the dance?
    Will you, won't you, will you, won't you,
    Will you join the dance?
    Will you, won't you, will you, won't you,
    Won't you join the dance?

'You can really have no notion
How delightful it will be,
When they take us up and throw us,
With the lobsters, out to sea!'
But the snail replied, 'Too far, too far!'
And gave a look askance,
Said he thanked the whiting kindly,
But he would not join the dance.
    Would not, could not, would not, could not,
    Would not join the dance,
    Would not, could not, would not, could not,
    Could not join the dance.

'What matters it how far we go?'
His scaly friend replied.
'There is another shore, you know,
Upon the other side.
The further off from England
The nearer is to France—
Then turn not pale, beloved snail,
But come and join the dance.
    Will you, won't you, will you, won't you,
    Will you join the dance?
    Will you, won't you, will you, won't you,
    Won't you join the dance?'

Lewis Carroll

Fairy Story

I went into the wood one day
And there I walked and lost my way

When it was so dark I could not see
A little creature came to me

He said if I would sing a song
The time would not be very long

But first I must let him hold my hand tight
Or else the wood would give me a fright

I sang a song, he let me go
But now I am home again there is nobody I know.

Stevie Smith

Up in a Basket

There was an old woman tossed up in a basket,
    Seventeen times as high as the moon;
And where she was going, I couldn't but ask it,
    For in her hand she carried a broom.
Old woman, old woman, old woman, quoth I,
    O whither, O whither, O whither so high?
To sweep the cobwebs off the sky!
    Shall I go with you? Aye, by-and-by.

Anonymous

The Hippopotamus

The huge hippopotamus hasn't a hair
on the back of his wrinkly hide;
he carries the bulk of his prominent hulk
rather loosely assembled inside.

The huge hippopotamus lives without care
at a slow philosophical pace,
as he wades in the mud with a thump and a thud
and a permanent grin on his face.

Jack Prelutsky

The Duck

Behold the duck.
It does not cluck.
A cluck it lacks.
It quacks.
It is specially fond
Of a puddle or pond.
When it dines or sups,
It bottoms ups.

Ogden Nash

The Owl and the Pussy-Cat

The Owl and the Pussy-Cat went to sea
    In a beautiful pea-green boat,
They took some honey, and plenty of money,
    Wrapped up in a five-pound note.
The Owl looked up to the stars above,
    And sang to a small guitar,
'O lovely Pussy! O Pussy, my love,
    What a beautiful Pussy you are,
        You are,
        You are!
    What a beautiful Pussy you are!'

Pussy said to the Owl, 'You elegant fowl!
  How charmingly sweet you sing!
O let us be married! too long we have tarried:
  But what shall we do for a ring?'
They sailed away, for a year and a day,
  To the land where the Bong-Tree grows,
And there in a wood a Piggy-wig stood,
  With a ring at the end of his nose,
    His nose,
    His nose,
  With a ring at the end of his nose.

'Dear Pig, are you willing to sell for one shilling
  Your ring?' Said the Piggy, 'I will.'
So they took it away, and were married next day
  By the Turkey who lives on the hill.
They dined on mince, and slices of quince,
  Which they ate with a runcible spoon;
And hand in hand, on the edge of the sand,
  They danced by the light of the moon,
    The moon,
    The moon,
  They danced by the light of the moon.

Edward Lear

Bedtime

The evening is coming,
The sun sinks to rest;
The rooks are all flying
Straight home to the nest.
'Caw!' says the rook, as he flies overhead;
'It's time little people were going to bed!'

The flowers are closing;
The daisy's asleep;
The primrose is buried
In slumber so deep.
Shut up for the night is the pimpernel red;
It's time little people were going to bed!

The butterfly, drowsy,
Has folded its wing;
The bees are returning;
No more the birds sing—
Their labour is over, their nestlings are fed;
It's time little people were going to bed!

Here comes the pony—
His work is all done;
Down through the meadow
He takes a good run;
Up go his heels, and down goes his head;
It's time little people were going to bed!

Good-night, little people,
Good-night, and good-night;
Sweet dreams to your eyelids
Till dawning of light;
The evening has come, there's no more to be said;
It's time little people were going to bed!

Thomas Hood